Hurricanes Have Eyes But Can't See

AND OTHER AMAZING FACTS ABOUT WILD WEATHER

by Melvin and Gilda Berger

SCHOLASTIC INC.

New York   Toronto   London   Auckland   Sydney
Mexico City   New Delhi   Hong Kong   Buenos Aires

ISBN 0-439-62534-3

12 11 10 9   10 11 12 13 14/0

Printed in the U.S.A.
First trade printing, August 2004
Interior art by Rémy Simard
Design by Janet Kusmierski
Photo research by Sarah Longacre

To Matt, a great guy

°C = degrees Celsius

cm = centimeter

g = gram

km = kilometer

km^2 = kilometers square

kph = kilometers per hour

kps = kilometers per second

m = meter

t = metric ton

INTRODUCTION

Hurricanes Have Eyes But Can't See takes a close-up look at wild weather.

Thunderstorms, hurricanes, tornadoes, blizzards, and other kinds of violent storms can do terrible damage. They can cause car, train, ship, and plane wrecks. They can smash windows, blow off roofs of houses, and flood cities. They can injure and sometimes kill people. And they can stop the flow of daily life.

It's often said, "Everyone talks about the weather, but no one does anything about it." That's true—you can't change the weather. But you can learn about it. You can find out what makes wild weather, what happens during big storms, how weather experts now warn and protect people, and what you can do to keep safe.

Hurricanes Have Eyes But Can't See has some amazing facts about wild weather. Did you know that

- a thunderstorm defeated Napoleon,

- a tornado blew a railroad car off its track,

- hurricane winds can blow up to 200 miles per hour (322 kph),

- an ice storm froze thousands of birds to death, and

- a hailstorm had stones as big as grapefruits?

Hold on to your hat—the information in this book may blow you away!

THUNDERSTORMS
What Is a Thunderstorm?

Thunderstorms are the most common wild-weather system. Thunderstorms are big and powerful. Heavy raindrops strike the ground. Strong winds whip across the land, scooping up dirt and litter. Bolts of lightning flash through the air. The ground shakes with the roar of thunder.

Speedy Fact 1

There are about 50,000 thunderstorms all over the world every day.

Speedy Fact 2

Thunderstorm raindrops are big—about 0.2 inches (0.5 cm) across. They fall at a speed of about 20 feet (6 m) per second.

Speedy Fact 3

High-flying clouds are a sign that a storm may be coming in twelve to twenty-four hours.

HOW BIG ARE WEATHER EVENTS?

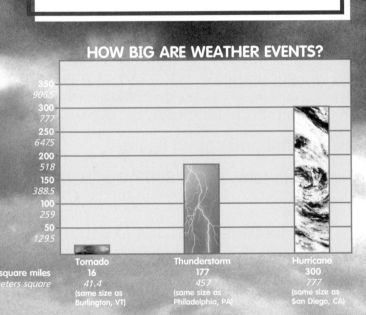

	350 / 906.5		
	300 / 777		
	250 / 6475		
	200 / 518		
	150 / 388.5		
	100 / 259		
	50 / 129.5		
	Tornado	**Thunderstorm**	**Hurricane**
square miles	16	177	300
kilometers square	41.4	457	777
	(same size as Burlington, VT)	(same size as Philadelphia, PA)	(same size as San Diego, CA)

High-flying Clouds

Cirrus   Cirrostratus   Cirrostratus

Before

During

After

Life of a Thunderstorm

Most thunderstorms are born on summer afternoons when the sun warms moist air at the earth's surface. The warm air rises and cools. Tiny drops of water gather in giant, dark clouds, called thunderheads. Rain starts to fall from the thunderhead. Lightning and thunder flash, crash, and roar.

A thunderstorm rages from about twenty minutes to an hour or more. The storm gradually quiets down. Soon the wind, rain, lightning, and thunder stop. The sun comes out. The thunderstorm is over.

HEIGHT OF CLOUDS ABOVE EARTH

	Stratus	Stratocumulus	Altocumulus	Thunderhead	Cirrocumulus	Cirrus
miles	less than 1	1	1.8	4.7	6.6	9.5
kilometers	less than 16	16	3	76	106	15

Speedy Fact 1

The bottom of a thunderhead is flat. It may be as low as 500 feet (152 m)—half the height of the Empire State Building.

Speedy Fact 2

The center of a thunderhead is less than 5 miles (8 km) above the earth's surface. Other clouds are higher or lower.

Speedy Fact 3

The upper parts of thunderhead clouds look like giant white castles piled on top of one another.

Speedy Fact 4

If all the clouds were to change to rain, the entire earth would be covered with 1 inch (2.5 cm) of water.

9

When and Where

Thunderstorms appear everywhere on earth. Most occur in parts of the world where the climate is warm and damp. The fewest number of storms appear in cold, dry regions. Some tropical regions in Africa get thunderstorms five days a week!

In the United States, thunderstorms are mostly found over cities and plains along the southern Atlantic coast and in the southwestern mountains. They generally strike during the summer.

Speedy Fact 1

The polar regions are too cold and dry for thunderstorms. They get only one every few years.

Speedy Fact 2

The island of Java in Indonesia holds the world record for the most thunderstorms. It has thunderstorms about 322 days a year.

Speedy Fact 3

In the United States, Florida holds the record for thunderstorms. Some parts of Florida get more than one hundred storms every year.

PACIFIC OCEAN

Java

There are about ten million lightning strikes throughout the world every day.

Lightning

Lightning is a bright, giant spark of electricity that jumps between a cloud and the ground, between two clouds, or within a cloud.

Inside a thunderhead, powerful winds cause drops of water and ice crystals to rub against one another. This creates an electrical charge that grows bigger and bigger. Soon, it is strong enough to make the electricity jump from one place to another. This makes a giant zigzag spark—a streak of lightning.

Lightning is five times hotter than the surface of the sun. It is hot enough to set a tree on fire.

Lightning between a cloud and earth can be 8 miles (13 km) long. Lightning between two clouds can be even longer.

Each bolt of lightning has an electrical charge of about thirty million volts. That's enough electricity to light up a small town for several months.

A bolt of lightning speeds through the air at about 78,000 miles per second (125,500 kps).

Thunder

Thunder always follows lightning. As lightning flashes through the air, it instantly heats the air to 54,000° Fahrenheit (30,000°C). The heated air explodes. It makes a loud crack of thunder, called a thunderclap.

After the thunderclap, the sound continues as a rumbling, rolling roar. The noise may be loud enough to shake windows and rattle dishes.

Speedy Fact 1

You don't hear most of the thunder's roar. It is too low in pitch for your ears.

Speedy Fact 2

The thunder that you hear is usually between 7 miles (11 km) and 20 miles (32 km) away.

HOW FAR FROM YOU IS THUNDER?

4 seconds				
3 seconds				
2 seconds				
1 second				
miles	.2	.4	.6	.8
kilometers	.3	.7	1.0	1.3

Speedy Fact 3

To find the distance between you and thunder, count the seconds between the lightning and the thunder (one one-thousand, two one-thousand, three one-thousand, and so on). Then divide the number of seconds by five. (Divide by three for kilometers.)

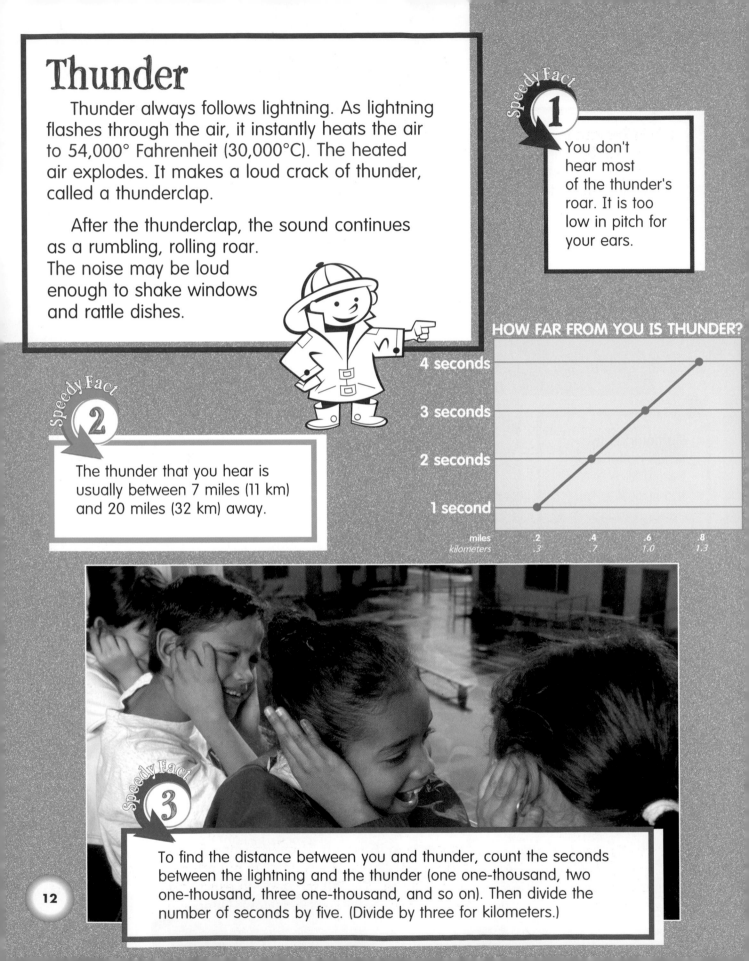

Record Thunderstorms

The most damaging thunderstorms are those with the heaviest rain and the most lightning. A sudden downpour of rain can wash away houses and roads and damage crops. Lightning may burn or kill people or start fires.

Sometimes, a single thunderstorm will split into two parts. Later, each part can split again. In this way, a single thunderstorm can turn into several storms that are usually severe.

Speedy Fact 1

Edwin Robinson was struck by lightning on June 4, 1980. Two months later, hair started growing on his bald head. No one knows why.

Speedy Fact 2

The deadliest thunderstorm came in 1856. Lightning struck a building filled with gunpowder on the island of Rhodes. The powerful blast killed 4,000 people.

Speedy Fact 3

In 1939, five German glider pilots parachuted inside a thunderhead. Four froze to death; only one survived.

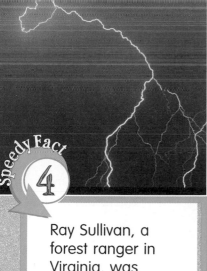

Speedy Fact 4

Ray Sullivan, a forest ranger in Virginia, was struck by lightning an amazing seven times between 1942 and 1977. He survived all seven strikes!

Speedy Fact 5

On June 18, 1815, a thunderstorm muddied the battlefield at Waterloo. This forced the French general, Napoleon Bonaparte, to put off his attack on the British. The British used the extra time to send in more troops—and defeat Napoleon.

13

Safety Tips

If you're outdoors during a thunderstorm, you can expect to get soaking wet. The scariest part may be the roar of thunder. But the most dangerous part is the lightning.

The chance of being hit by lightning is very small. Some say it is less than your chance of winning the lottery. Yet lightning can hurt you. It is wise to remember the speedy facts below on how to keep safe in a thunderstorm.

Speedy Fact 1

Keep away from tall trees standing alone. When lightning strikes, it usually hits the highest object.

Speedy Fact 2

If you are swimming, get out of the water. Water is an excellent conductor of electricity.

Speedy Fact 3

Don't touch a stove, metal fence, or railing. Metals conduct lightning.

Speedy Fact 4

Don't use the telephone or television during a thunderstorm. The wires could bring lightning into your house.

Speedy Fact 5

If you are in a car, stay there. If lightning hits, the car will pass the electricity safely into the ground.

MONSOONS
What Is a Monsoon?

Monsoons are strong winds that blow from tropical seas toward land during the summer. Monsoons are also storms—usually without thunder or lightning—that dump huge amounts of rain on the land.

Monsoons mostly occur in areas near the equator. The summer sun heats the land more than it heats the sea. The hot, dry air over the land rises. Cool, damp air from over the sea rushes in to take its place. The dampness produces the monsoon rains that fall without stopping for weeks or months.

Speedy Fact 1

Monsoons are strongest in southern Asia. But they also bring heavy rain to parts of the southern United States, Australia, and Africa.

Speedy Fact 2

Monsoon rains fall during the six months between April and October.

Speedy Fact 3

Farmers need the monsoon rains to grow their crops. People in India greet the start of the rainy season with a happy festival called *Teej*.

Speedy Fact 4

In some places, monsoons cause yearly floods. To stay dry, some people build their houses on stilts.

HURRICANES
What Is a Hurricane?

A hurricane is a huge, doughnut-shaped storm with heavy rain and strong winds swirling around a calm center. Hurricanes are the biggest and most destructive of all storms. The small, calm center, where no rain falls and the winds are quiet, is called the *eye* of the hurricane.

A hurricane has winds greater than 74 miles per hour (116 kph). If the winds are less than this, it is called a *tropical storm*.

Speedy Fact 1
An average hurricane is about 300 miles (480 km) across. The eye is usually about 20 miles (32 km) wide.

Speedy Fact 2
Huge amounts of rain fall during a hurricane. An average hurricane raises the water level in a swimming pool about 9 inches (23 cm).

Speedy Fact 3
The strongest winds of a hurricane have been measured at 200 miles per hour (322 kph).

Speedy Fact 4
The word *hurricane* may come from an old West Indian word that means *big wind*, or from the Spanish word for hurricane, *huracàn*.

Life of a Hurricane

Hurricanes begin over ocean waters when the air is warm and there is a lot of moisture in the air. The warm, moist air rises. Cold air rushes in, forming big, swirling clouds. Soon, rain comes pouring down and powerful winds whip through the air. It's a hurricane!

Pounding rain and strong winds—often with thunder and lightning—move through the area. Suddenly, the air grows quiet as the eye of the hurricane passes overhead. Then the other part of the storm arrives. This time, though, the winds blow from the opposite direction. About five hours later, the hurricane begins to fade away.

When and Where

Most hurricanes form in broad belts on both sides of the equator. The storms usually strike north of the equator, from June through November, and south of the equator, from November through June. That is when the surface of the water is warmest.

At first, hurricanes were named for saints. Later, they were given girls' names. Today, the National Hurricane Center alternates girls' and boys' names in alphabetical order for Atlantic hurricanes. At the beginning of the season, they start all over again with the letter A.

Hurricanes are known by different names around the world. In China and Japan, they are called *typhoons*. If they appear in the Indian Ocean, they're called *tropical cyclones*. Australians call them *willy-willies*.

Speedy Fact 1

Hurricanes usually form within 1,000 miles (1,600 km) north or south of the equator.

Speedy Fact 3

Florida and Texas are struck by hurricanes coming from the east. In the Gulf of Mexico and on the East Coast, the storms almost always come from the south.

Speedy Fact 2

The longest-lasting hurricane in the Atlantic Ocean was Hurricane Ginger in 1971. It lasted 20 days.

Speedy Fact 4

Hurricane hunters fly their airplanes into hurricanes. They measure a storm's size, location, speed, and direction.

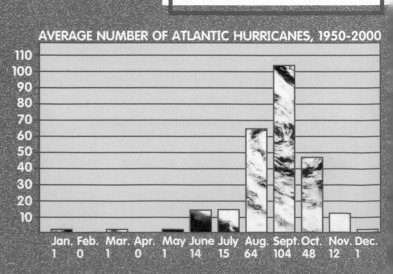

AVERAGE NUMBER OF ATLANTIC HURRICANES, 1950-2000

Jan.	Feb.	Mar.	Apr.	May	June	July	Aug.	Sept.	Oct.	Nov.	Dec.
1	0	1	0	1	14	15	64	104	48	12	1

Storm Surge

A storm surge is a sharp rise of ocean water due to a hurricane. Hurricane winds push the water higher and higher, much like a snowplow makes a hill of snow.

Storm surges cause the most damage during a hurricane. A huge wall of water sweeps over beaches and low-lying land. It washes away everything in its path. Also, the ocean water that floods the land stays onshore long after the hurricane is gone. The saltwater kills growing plants and makes the soil unfit for future crops. Often, the seawater gets into wells, making the water unfit to drink.

Speedy Fact 1

The water level of the ocean during a storm surge may rise 25 feet (8 m). That's higher than a two-story building!

Speedy Fact 2

The highest-known storm surge was in Bathurst Bay, Australia. There, the water rose to the height of a four-story building.

Speedy Fact 3

About nine out of every ten deaths during hurricanes are drownings caused by storm surges.

Speedy Fact 4

Hurricane Camille hit Mississippi in August 1969. Its storm surge pushed onshore several huge ships. Other storm surges have carried boats nearly 0.5 mile (0.8 km) inland.

Record Hurricanes

Hurricanes are very dangerous storms. High winds, pelting rain, and storm surges topple trees, destroy buildings, wreck cars, tear down telephone lines, and fling pieces of wreckage. Ships at sea are sunk; boats along the coast are flung onto the land.

The worst hurricane year in the United States was 1955. Twelve major hurricanes struck, leaving about 1,500 people dead and destroying $2 billion worth of property. The best year was 1983, when only four hurricanes passed over the United States.

Speedy Fact 1

No one knows the wind strength of Hurricane Camille, which occurred in August 1969. The winds knocked out many of the measuring instruments.

Speedy Fact 2

The hurricane that killed the most people hit the Bay of Bengal in November 1970. It sent a storm surge onto the land, which left about 300,000 dead.

Speedy Fact 3

Hurricane Andrew, in August 1992, was the worst single hurricane to strike the United States. Property damage was more than $46 billion.

During a hurricane, stay indoors and away from windows.

Beware the eye, or center, of the storm. A hurricane is not over until the second half of the hurricane passes by.

Safety Tips

In the past, hurricanes have caught people without warning. As a result, many lost their property and even their lives.

Today, the National Hurricane Center watches out for hurricanes. They use satellites, radar, hurricane hunter planes, and advanced measuring instruments to track storms. They warn people about when and where hurricanes may hit.

If you live in an area that gets hurricanes, listen to the radio or watch television during hurricane season. A *hurricane watch* means that a hurricane might reach land within two days. A *hurricane warning* means that a hurricane is expected within twenty-four hours.

Before a hurricane occurs, tape or board up windows, pick up outdoor objects that might blow around, and prepare a battery-operated radio and flashlights.

If you are outdoors, stay away from downed wires and broken glass. Don't get in the way of first-aid and rescue workers.

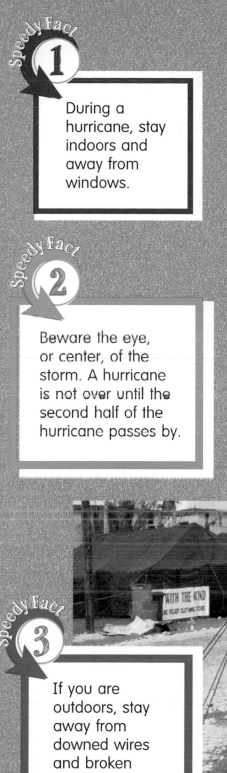

American Red Cross

DISASTER SERVICES

TORNADOES
What Is a Tornado?

A tornado is a small but very violent storm. No weather system on earth has faster-blowing winds. Because of its spinning winds, a tornado is often called a *twister*.

A tornado is like a thunderstorm. But in a tornado, the rising air inside the big, dark thunderhead forms a twirling funnel. The funnel, which is between 800 and 2,000 feet (244 and 610 m) tall and from 10 feet (3 m) to slightly more than 1 mile (1.6 km) wide, reaches from the cloud down to the ground. Some say it looks like a giant elephant's trunk swinging back and forth.

Speedy Fact 1

Tornado winds spin at more than 124 miles per hour (200 kph) and move across the land at about 35 miles per hour (56 kph).

Speedy Fact 2

Tornadoes make as much noise as one hundred jumbo jets taking off at the same time.

Speedy Fact 3

At first, tornado funnels are clear or white in color. But when they touch the ground, the funnels turn black or dark gray because of the dirt, dust, and debris they sweep up.

Speedy Fact 4

In 1755, Benjamin Franklin chased on horseback a small tornado for nearly 1 mile (1.6 km). He kept trying to break up the storm by lashing out at it with his whip.

Tornadoes almost always grow out of thunderstorms, but not all thunderstorms lead to tornadoes.

Life of a Tornado

A tornado usually begins in an area where a layer of warm, moist air is covered by a layer of cool, dry air. The hot air rises and the cool air works its way down. This forms a thunderhead cloud. Strong, fast winds start to blow. The winds spin and whirl around like water going down a bathtub drain. It's a tornado!

The tornado rushes forward, lifting or wrecking everything in its path. Within an hour—and usually much sooner—the fury of the tornado is over. But watch out. As the tornado fades away, other tornadoes may form and grow.

NORTH
AMERICA
U.S.
ATLANTIC
OCEAN
CENTRAL
AMERICA
PACIFIC
OCEAN
SOUTH
AMERICA

South of the equator, most tornado winds twist clockwise. North of the equator, most twist counterclockwise.

In May 1881, a tornado off the coast of England sucked up hundreds of crabs from the water. When the storm slowed down, it rained crabs.

An average tornado follows a path that is no more than 16 miles (26 km) long.

The record life of a tornado is nine hours.

Before

During

After

When and Where

Tornadoes strike every continent on earth. But more tornadoes happen in the United States than anywhere else. Most occur in the Tornado Alley, a stretch of land that runs from Texas to Nebraska. Here, warm, wet air from the Gulf of Mexico meets cold air from central Canada and dry air from the western part of the United States.

Tornadoes happen all year long, but most strike between April and June. Tornadoes usually start in the late afternoon, the warmest time of the day. The largest number touch down between 4:00 and 6:00 P.M.

Speedy Fact 1

Texas gets more tornadoes than any other state.

Speedy Fact 2

An average of 800 tornadoes occur every year in the United States. In spring 1974, there were 90 tornadoes in just one day— a record number!

Speedy Fact 3

In 1957, a very powerful tornado in Dallas, Texas, had the fastest winds. They reached an estimated 310 miles per hour (500 kph).

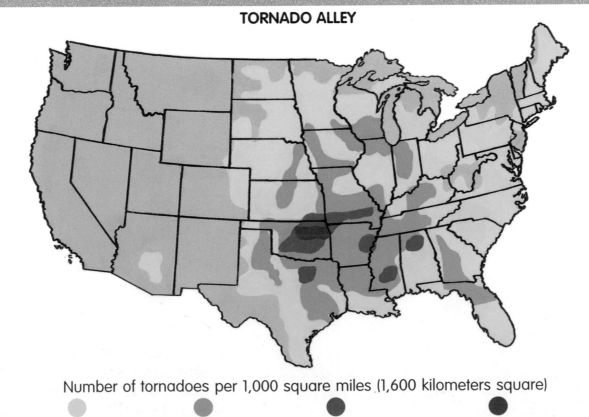

TORNADO ALLEY

Number of tornadoes per 1,000 square miles (1,600 kilometers square)

1-5 tornadoes　　6-10 tornadoes　　11-15 tornadoes　　more than 15 tornadoes

Waterspouts

Sometimes the whirling winds of a tornado form over a lake or an ocean. They may form a tall, thin column of water called a *waterspout*. The water comes from moisture in the air, not from the water in the lake or ocean. The waterspout may reach all the way up to the bottom of a cloud.

A single waterspout usually causes little damage. Its winds are frequently less than 50 miles per hour (80 kph). Most die away in about 15 minutes. Occasionally, two or three waterspouts form at the same time, right next to each other. These waterspouts may cause more damage.

Speedy Fact 1

While most waterspouts form over water, others are tornadoes that move from land to water.

Speedy Fact 2

Waterspouts die if they pass from water to land.

Speedy Fact 3

Waterspouts form year-round in warm climates. In cooler areas, they just happen in the summer.

Speedy Fact 4

Most waterspouts in the United States occur in the waters around the Florida Keys or the Great Lakes.

Record Tornadoes

Until 1953, the average yearly death toll in the United States from tornadoes was 230. But much-improved tracking, measuring, and communication systems have cut the death toll to about 100 per year. Worldwide, the single worst death toll was on April 26, 1989, when a tornado in Bangladesh left 1,300 dead.

The worst tornado in United States history swept from Missouri to Indiana on March 18, 1925. It lasted 3.5 hours and took 689 lives.

Speedy Fact 1

A twister on May 26, 1917, had the longest path on record. It smashed through the states of Missouri, Illinois, and Indiana—a 293-mile-long (471 km) trip.

Speedy Fact 2

A cluster of 148 tornadoes on April 3-4, 1974, tore through thirteen states.

Speedy Fact 3

A tornado on June 23, 1944, blew out all the water in the West Fork River in West Virginia for a few minutes.

Speedy Fact 4

A powerful tornado struck near Moorhead, Minnesota, on May 27, 1931. The storm lifted an 83-ton (84.3 t) railroad car with 117 passengers off the tracks and dropped it into a ditch 80 feet (24 m) away.

Speedy Fact 5

In Italy, a tornado in September 1981 hoisted a carriage with a sleeping baby, carried it nearly 330 feet (101 m), and set it down so smoothly that the baby didn't even wake up.

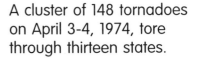

If you're outdoors at the start of a tornado, hurry to the nearest basement. If this is not possible, lie flat in a ditch or on the ground. Cover your head with your hands to protect yourself from flying debris.

Safety Tips

Tornadoes can be very dangerous. The first warning usually comes on the radio or television. Weather scientists issue a *tornado watch*, which tells you that a tornado may develop in the next few hours. This may be followed by a *tornado warning*, which means a tornado has been seen or picked up on radar.

Scientists track the tornado with their instruments. Sometimes they get in cars and follow the storm, checking the tornado's wind speed, direction, and path.

If you're indoors, head to the basement or crouch inside a closet or bathroom. Keep away from windows, metal things, and anything that uses electricity.

If you're in a car, don't try to outrace the storm. Get out of the vehicle and either find shelter or fall to the ground.

BLIZZARDS
What Is a Blizzard?

A blizzard is a severe storm that combines heavy snowfall with low temperatures and strong winds. The falling and blowing snow during a blizzard makes it very hard to see. The very frigid temperature makes it so cold that your ears, nose, fingers, and toes can freeze, which is called *frostbite*.

During a true blizzard, the temperature is below 20° Fahrenheit (-6°C). Winds blow at least 35 miles per hour (60 kph). And you can see no farther than .25 mile (0.4 km)—that's about five city blocks.

Speedy Fact 1
Blizzards last anywhere from a few hours to a few days.

Speedy Fact 2
In a blizzard, snowflakes fall at the rate of 2 inches (5 cm) per hour.

Speedy Fact 3
Many blizzards come after a period of very warm weather in winter.

Speedy Fact 4
In case of frostbite, cover the damaged area with extra clothes or a blanket. If possible, warm your body with warm—not hot—water.

Life of a Blizzard

Most blizzards begin when a mass of cold air moves out of the Arctic and toward an area with warm, mild air. The cold air mass bumps into the warm air. Heavy snow falls along the line where the two air masses meet. The temperature drops and powerful winds swirl. It's a blizzard!

During a blizzard, schools, stores, and factories close. Cars, trucks, planes, and trains stop moving. Telephones don't work, and some areas lose electricity. After several hours or a few days, the worst is over. Often, the sun comes out. Everything looks beautiful under a blanket of clean, white snow.

Speedy Fact

1

In the United States, the warm air that makes a blizzard may come from over the Atlantic Ocean, the Gulf of Mexico, or both.

Speedy Fact

2

Most blizzards move from west to east. This is the opposite of hurricanes, which usually move from east to west.

Speedy Fact

3

Sometimes winds whip heavy amounts of snow around so that it looks white in every direction. This is called a *whiteout*.

Speedy Fact

4

The worst whiteouts are found in the polar regions. They are mostly caused by ice on the ground and blowing snow.

Speedy Fact

5

Penguins in Antarctica stand on the ice with their backs turned against the blizzard winds.

When and Where

Blizzards only strike areas where it is cold enough to snow. They mostly occur in the polar regions, in the central and eastern parts of the United States and Canada, and in Russia. They rarely appear in warmer southern areas.

Most blizzards occur in winter or early spring. Many are brought in by strong winds known as *northeasters*, or *nor'easters*. The winds form over the Atlantic Ocean and dump gigantic amounts of snow along the East Coast of the United States.

RUSSIA

CANADA

U.S.

Speedy Fact 1

The blizzard of 1888 dropped 50 inches (1.27 m) of snow in places on the East Coast of the United States.

Speedy Fact 2

The temperatures in the eastern and central parts of the United States hit record lows during a blizzard in January 1979.

Speedy Fact 3

The most snow in a single storm fell on Mount Shasta in California on February 13-14, 1959. It piled up 189 inches (473 cm), which is higher than a basketball hoop.

Some avalanches spill down the mountain at speeds of about 225 miles per hour (362 kph). That's as fast as a race car.

Avalanches

An avalanche is a rush of snow down a mountain. It often comes after a severe blizzard has dumped a tremendous amount of snow on the mountainside.

About 1,200 avalanches are reported in the United States every year. Most occur when loose, powdery snow falls on top of hard, icy, older snow. The top layers break free and sweep down the slope, destroying everything in their path.

Avalanches do not kill many people. That's because most avalanches occur on mountains where few people live.

A large avalanche moves enough snow to cover 20 football fields with 10 feet (3 m) of snow.

The ringing bells of Switzerland's Church of St. Nicolas started an avalanche in 1749. The avalanche swept away the church, but it didn't harm the separate bell tower.

In the Swiss mountains, St. Bernard dogs were trained to rescue people buried in avalanches.

Record Blizzards

The most famous blizzard in the United States was the blizzard of 1888. From March 11-14, 1888, the blizzard stormed over the eastern part of the country. The heavy snowfall and winds up to 48 miles per hour (77 kph) knocked out electricity and telephones in Washington, D.C., Philadelphia, New York, and Boston. Two hundred ships sank or were badly damaged in the Atlantic Ocean. Four hundred people lost their lives.

Speedy Fact 1

Gusts of wind during the blizzard of 1888 piled the snow in New York City high enough to cover four-story buildings.

Speedy Fact 2

After the blizzard of 1888, a man put a funny sign in the pile of snow in front of his store: THIS SNOW IS FREE. TAKE A SAMPLE.

Speedy Fact 3

The worst blizzard since 1888 happened in March 1993, in the eastern United States. Winds howled with a force of more than 75 miles per hour (121 kph).

Safety Tips

Severe blizzards still happen. But today weather scientists can tell us when to expect them. The National Weather Service broadcasts a *snow watch* 12 to 36 hours before they expect 6 inches (15 cm) or more of snow. They issue a *snow warning* 12 to 18 hours before they think the snowfall will begin.

The major causes of deaths during a blizzard are car crashes, heart attacks while shoveling snow, getting lost, and freezing to death.

Speedy Fact 1

If you live in an area that gets blizzards, always keep a supply of canned food and bottled water, as well as a battery-operated radio, in your home.

Speedy Fact 2

You should have in your car plenty of gas, extra clothing, a blanket, food, water, and a snow shovel.

Speedy Fact 5

If you get lost during a blizzard, lie down in the snow. The blanket of snow traps a layer of warm air around your body. But make sure to poke a hole in the snow for air. This is how polar bears survive in the snow.

Speedy Fact 3

Roads are more dangerous at the beginning of a blizzard because they are most slippery with a thin coating of snow.

Speedy Fact 4

If you must go out in a blizzard, wear several layers of warm clothing, including a hat. Cover as much of your skin as possible to avoid frostbite.

RAINSTORMS
What Is a Rainstorm?

A rainstorm is a heavy rainfall. The tiny drops of water that make up clouds keep bumping into each other. Some drops stick together to form larger drops. After millions of collisions, the raindrops grow very big and they fall to earth. If enough rain falls, it's a rainstorm.

Rainstorms drop a tremendous amount of water on earth. Experts say that an average rainstorm dumps 7 inches (17.8 cm) of rain on the ground.

Speedy Fact 1

Heavy or long rainstorms can cause floods.

Speedy Fact 2

Raindrops are shaped like tiny, flat hamburger buns—not like tears or pears, as often shown.

Speedy Fact 3

It takes about one million drops of water in a cloud to make just one raindrop.

Speedy Fact 4

At the center of every raindrop is either a speck of dust or a very small ice crystal.

HANNIBAL
WATER WORKS

When and Where

Rain falls everywhere on earth, but not in equal amounts. Deserts never get rainstorms. Rain forests and places on both sides of the equator get the most rain. The rest of the earth gets a moderate amount of rain.

Heavy rainstorms caused the giant Mississippi River to flood in 1993. The water covered parts of 9 states and destroyed the homes of 45,000 families.

Scientists now know when and where floods may occur. They alert people to the danger. But many still settle in these places. That's because flooding often makes land fertile and good for growing crops.

Speedy Fact 1

On March 14-15, 1952, Réunion Island in the Indian Ocean set a record with 73.62 inches (187 cm) of rain in just two days. It takes two years for that much rain to fall in Dallas, Texas.

Speedy Fact 2

Several rainstorms over Johnstown, Pennsylvania, in May 1889, caused the most famous American flood. A burst dam released floodwaters that leveled every building.

Speedy Fact 3

Rain forests get an average of about 21 feet (6.4 m) of rain every year. The yearly average for the rest of the earth is only 3 feet (1 m).

P.R.R.

ICE STORMS
What Is an Ice Storm?

An ice storm occurs when drops of rain are cooled as they fall through cold air. The drops freeze when they hit the ground, trees, buildings, and power lines. The freezing rain covers everything with a thin—or thick—coating of ice.

Perhaps the worst ice storm in the United States came in the winter of 1951, when some 5 inches (12.7 cm) of rain fell. It covered 8 southeastern states with 3 to 4 inches (7.5 to 10 cm) of ice.

Speedy Fact 1

Ice storms never strike the polar regions. It is too cold for rain to fall.

Speedy Fact 2

More than 80 percent of deaths from ice storms are caused by cars skidding on icy roads.

Speedy Fact 3

There is a three-to-one chance that the New England area will have at least one ice storm every winter.

Ice-storm Damage

Ice-storm damage occurs in a few ways. The ice coats the roads and sidewalks so that cars skid and people slip and fall. This leads to many injuries.

The heavy ice snaps telephone poles and breaks the power wires they carry. This cuts off electricity and telephone service to homes. Fallen electrical wires give dangerous shocks to anyone who touches them. Airplane travel also suffers delays while planes are de-iced before takeoff.

Speedy Fact 1

Many wild birds and animals freeze to death during ice storms. Others starve because they can't fly or move to find food.

Speedy Fact 2

During a typical ice storm, a 50-foot (15 m) pine tree can be coated with ice that weighs 5 tons (5.5 t).

Speedy Fact 3

In a 1961 ice storm in Idaho, the ice was as thick as 8 inches (20.3 cm).

Speedy Fact 4

Ice storms damage old trees more than young ones, and tall trees more than short ones.

STOP

DROUGHTS
What Is a Drought?

A drought is a period of time when an area gets less rain and snow than normal. Deserts get very little rain and snow—but that is normal and not a drought.

Droughts are usually caused by major changes in weather patterns. A long heat wave can produce a drought. A change in the usual flow of winds is another cause. A current of warm water in the Pacific Ocean, called El Niño, sometimes leads to droughts.

Speedy Fact 1

A drought is defined in different ways around the world.

Speedy Fact 2

Unlike most wild weather, droughts happen gradually. It usually takes weeks or months before people know there is a drought.

Speedy Fact 3

In times of drought, scientists sometimes hurl different chemicals into the clouds to try and make it rain.

Speedy Fact 4

Calama, Chile had the longest drought—400 years. A rainstorm finally came on February 10, 1972. Floods destroyed every building.

WHAT IS A DROUGHT?

	Australia (less than 10% of normal rainfall for the year)	India (less than 75% of normal rainfall for the year)	United States (less than 30% of normal rainfall for 3 weeks)
75%			
50%			
25%			

Drought Damage

Droughts cause many problems. People don't have enough water for drinking, cooking, or bathing. Farm crops wilt and die. Both farm animals and wild animals can die of thirst and hunger.

Drought also dries up the topsoil. It turns rich soil into a dusty powder. Trees dry out, so they burn very easily. Either lightning or careless people start wildfires that can destroy whole forests.

Speedy Fact 1

You can trace the history of droughts in a tree's rings. The rings are thick during normal years and thin during drought years.

Speedy Fact 2

A study of tree rings at the University of Arizona showed that the drought there in the 1950s was the worst in 700 years.

Speedy Fact 3

One of the worst droughts in history happened in the southwestern part of the United States from 1931 to 1938. Farmers and ranchers were forced to move to other areas of the country.

Speedy Fact 4

So much soil was blown away during the 1931-1938 drought that the drought area became known as the Dust Bowl.

DUST STORMS
What Is a Dust Storm?

A dust storm is a huge wall of thick dust and dirt that blows across the ground. This often happens during a drought. The drought leaves the top layer of soil dry, loose, and easily blown away.

It is impossible to see very far while the dust storm is blowing. The National Weather Service says that when you cannot see more than .6 mile (1 km), it is a dust storm. It's called a severe dust storm if you can see only half that far.

Speedy Fact
1

Most dust storms come in the spring. One reason is because new crops are not yet able to hold down the soil.

Speedy Fact
2

The advancing wall of a dust storm can reach as high as a ten-story building.

Speedy Fact
3

Some dust storms can last for several days. The dust may be fine enough to work its way between the pages of a closed book.

Speedy Fact
4

Some dust storms can blow over thousands of miles (kilometers). They have been known to cross the ocean, from Australia all the way to New Zealand.

Dust Devils

Dust devils look like mini-tornadoes, but are not nearly as dangerous. They are really dust storms with whirling columns of air. Strong winds rise up in the center of these turning winds. The moving air picks up dry soil and dust and carries it up into the air.

Dust devils can rip roofs off houses and flip over parked cars, but they rarely harm people. That's because most dust devils move slowly. People usually have time to get out of the way.

Speedy Fact 1

Most dust devils form in hot deserts or drought areas, such as Australia, the southwestern part of the United States, and the Middle East.

Speedy Fact 2

Dust devils can rise 1,000 feet (300 m) to 2,500 feet (762 m) above the ground.

Speedy Fact 4

The winds in dust devils usually blow at less than 50 miles per hour (80 kph).

Speedy Fact 3

A big dust devil can be as wide as 280 feet (85 m).

HAILSTORMS
What Is a Hailstorm?

Hailstorms are storms in which big or small balls of ice, called *hailstones*, fall to the ground. The hailstones begin as frozen raindrops inside thunderstorm clouds. The winds blow the little hailstones up and down. Raindrops freeze on the hailstones, making them bigger and heavier. They grow until they are heavy enough to fall to earth.

Most hailstones are about the size of peas. But bigger ones are the size of golf balls, tennis balls, or even grapefruits.

Speedy Fact 1

Hailstorms grow out of thunderstorms. Most hailstorms last less than 10 minutes and cover only a small area.

Speedy Fact 2

When sliced open, every hailstone has a series of rings, like an onion. If you count the rings, you can tell how many times the hailstone went up and down in the thunderhead. The usual number ranges from three to twenty-five.

Speedy Fact 3

Big hailstones plunge down at about 100 miles per hour (160 kph).

Speedy Fact 4

A hailstone that landed near Vicksburg, Mississippi, on May 11, 1894, contained a turtle. Reports say that the turtle was alive and able to crawl away.

When and Where

In the United States, most hailstorms occur late in the afternoon or early evening during spring, summer, and fall. The Great Plains gets more hailstorms than any other part of the country. Elsewhere, hail falls in Argentina, northern Italy, Kenya, and South Africa.

Heavy hailstorms can cause great damage. They smash windows, dent cars, kill small animals like cats, dogs, and chickens, and ruin crops. Only the worst hailstorms, with giant hailstones, hurt people. The one known American death caused by hail was that of a farmer in Texas in 1931.

FOG
What Is Fog?

Fog is a cloud that is close to the ground. It usually forms when the air temperature at ground level drops at night or early in the morning. The cooling changes the moisture in the air into a cloud of tiny drops of water. When the sun rises and warms the air, the fog breaks up.

In true fog, it is possible to see a little over .6 mile (1 km) ahead. Fog that is not that thick is known as mist.

Speedy Fact 1
Fog does not form if the wind is blowing faster than 6 miles per hour (9.7 km).

Speedy Fact 2
Experts say the drops of water in fog are so tiny that it takes about seven trillion to make one tablespoon of water.

Speedy Fact 3
Sea fog appears along seacoasts when ocean breezes bring warm, moist air over cool land or cool water.

Speedy Fact 4
Sometimes fog combines with smoke in the air to form smog (combination of smoke and fog)—a kind of pollution.

Fog Damage

Fog is dangerous because it cuts the ability to see very far ahead. Cars, trucks, trains, and buses crash. Ships collide and sink. And airplanes slide off runways during takeoffs or landings.

The foggiest place in the United States is Libby Island, Maine. It has 1,554 hours of fog every year.

Speedy Fact 1

On July 25, 1956, two ships, the *Stockholm* and the *Andrea Doria*, collided in fog over the Atlantic Ocean. The *Andrea Doria* sank, taking 51 lives.

Speedy Fact 2

Fog has caused as many as one hundred cars to pile up in one highway accident.

Speedy Fact 3

In 1579, Sir Francis Drake and his crew sailed past San Francisco, but they did not see the harbor because of the fog.

Speedy Fact 4

The worst smog disaster struck London, England, in December 1952. Accidents and heart and lung disease killed about 4,000.

HEAT WAVES
What Is a Heat Wave?

A heat wave is a period of very hot weather. It usually lasts two or more days. During that time, there are few or no clouds, no rain, very dry air, and little wind.

Most heat waves come during the summer. That's when the long hours of sunshine and short hours of darkness give the air little chance to cool off.

Speedy Fact 1

Heat waves kill almost as many people as do blizzards.

Speedy Fact 2

During a heat wave you can sometimes fry eggs on the sidewalk.

Speedy Fact 3

Deserts around the world have heat waves almost all the time. The temperature during the summer is between 120° Fahrenheit (67°C) and 130° Fahrenheit (72°C).

Heat-wave Damage

Heat waves are dangerous to all—but especially the very young and the very old. Animals, too, fall ill or die during periods of very hot weather. And since it rarely rains during a heat wave, growing plants die from the high heat and lack of water.

One of the worst heat waves struck the city of Chicago in July 1995. The temperature rose as high as 106° Fahrenheit (41°C). In five days, it killed 525 people.

Speedy Fact 1

New York City had a severe heat wave on June 25-27, 1952. About 200 people died each day due to heat-related illnesses or accidents.

Speedy Fact 2

Large cities sometimes become *heat islands*. Buildings, streets, and paved parking lots give off heat. The added warmth can raise the temperature over a city as much as 15° Fahrenheit (8°C).

Speedy Fact 3

The highest United States temperature was 134° Fahrenheit (57°C), in Death Valley, California, on July 10, 1913. The streets were so hot that they melted the soles of people's sneakers.

FORECASTING WILD WEATHER

A number of scientists at the National Weather Service are experts in wild weather. They collect information from weather stations around the world. Satellites radio down reports on the weather from space. And ships and airplanes all over the globe let them know the weather conditions in their areas. These weather scientists then use the information to forecast changes in the weather.

Workers at the Storm Prediction Center in Norman, Oklahoma, study thunderstorms, tornadoes, blizzards, and rainstorms. They track these storms with radar. They launch planes and balloons to learn more about the weather conditions in and around storms.

The National Hurricane Center in Miami, Florida, is the home of hurricane experts. Like the scientists at the Science Prediction Center, they follow weather conditions around the world. They also send hurricane hunters to fly their planes through hurricanes. Their measuring instruments give them a very complete and exact picture of what goes on inside hurricanes.

When wild-weather scientists are certain that a storm will strike, they send out a storm warning. This usually tells us where the storm is headed, how strong it will be, and how long it will last. Often, the warning includes information on how to prepare for the storm and how to be safe during and after the storm.

We cannot do anything about the weather—but we can be watchful and well-informed. As Charles Dickens said: "There's something good in all weathers."